WPC

SEASONS

Autumn

Kay Barnham

WAYLAND

Explore the world with **Popcorn** - your complete first non-fiction library.

Look out for more titles in the **Popcorn** range. All books have the same format of simple text and awesome images. Text is carefully matched to the pictures to help readers to identify and understand key vocabulary. www.waylandbooks.co.uk/popcorn

First published in 2009 by Wayland

Copyright © Wayland 2009

Wayland
Hachette Children's Books
338 Euston Road
London NW1 3BH

Wayland Australia
Level 17/207 Kent Street
Sydney NSW 2000

Senior Editor: Claire Shanahan
Designer: Ruth Cowan
Picture Researcher: Louise Edgeworth
Concept Designer: Paul Cherrill

British Library Cataloguing in Publication Data:
Barnham, Kay
Autumn. - (Popcorn. Seasons)
1. Autumn - Juvenile literature
I. Title
508.2

ISBN: 978 07502 5789 3

Printed and bound in China

Wayland is a division of Hachette Children's Books, an Hachette UK Company.
www.hachette.co.uk

Acknowledgements:
Alamy: Dan O'Flynn Title page, Inga Spence Imprint page, Andre Jenny p4-5, Enigma p7, Steve Atkins p10, Dan O'Flynn p13, Grant Rooney p16, Inga Spence p17, Louise Batalla Duran p19; Corbis: Claude Woodruff COVER, p15; Getty Images: Schultheiss Selection GmbH & CoKG p9, p14, Mel Yates/Stone p18; Istockphoto: p6, Ina Peters p11, Nickolay Bolshackov p12.

Contents

The seasons   4

Autumn weather   6

Autumn trees   8

Autumn crops   10

Animals in autumn   12

Autumn fun   14

Autumn food   16

Autumn festivals   18

Why do we have seasons?   20

Make a bird-seed feeder   22

Glossary   24

Index   24

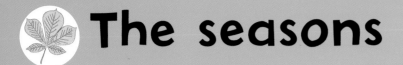

The seasons

There are four seasons in the year.
The seasons are called spring, summer,
autumn and winter. Each season is different.

In autumn, the days grow shorter.
The weather becomes cooler.
The autumn months are September,
October and November.

Autumn weather

In autumn, there are fewer dry, sunny days than in summer. Clouds hide the sun. Some days may be foggy.

There may even be frost at this time of year.

Blustery, cold and wet weather is common. You will need to wear clothes that keep you warm and dry.

In autumn, there may be strong winds and heavy rain.

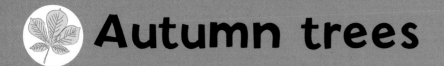

Autumn trees

Leaves turn sunlight into energy. This helps trees grow. When the weather is colder and cloudier in autumn, the leaves are not needed anymore. They fall from the trees.

Leaves change colour before they fall.

Trees also drop their seeds at this time of year. New trees will grow from these seeds in spring.

Horse chestnut trees have round shiny seeds called conkers.

 Autumn crops

Farmers plant seeds in spring. They grow crops of barley, wheat, corn and maize. By autumn, the crops are ready to be harvested.

The farmer is harvesting this field of wheat.

The grain from crops can be made into food for us to eat. Some of the grain is fed to farm animals.

Grain can be used to make bread.

Animals in autumn

In autumn, cats, dogs, foxes and squirrels
grow thicker coats. They are getting
ready for cold weather. Some birds
fly to warmer countries.

This dog's
thick coat will
keep it warm
during the colder
months.

Squirrels spend the autumn gathering
nuts. They hide the nuts in safe places,
so that they will have food to eat
in winter.

Autumn fun

The nights get longer and the days get shorter in autumn. But there is still enough daylight to have fun outdoors. Windy autumn weather is perfect for windsurfing and flying kites.

When it is windy, windsurfers can leap into the air!

Why not go on a nature walk?
You can collect crunchy leaves,
conkers and acorns.

How many different
coloured leaves
can you find?

15

Autumn food

Lots of different fruits are ripe in autumn. Blackberries grow in hedgerows. Orchards are full of apples, pears and plums.

These plums can be cooked in a pie.

Look out for ripe vegetables, too.
Mushrooms grow wild in fields.
Farmers and gardeners harvest
pumpkins, courgettes and leeks.

Can you think of a use for this ripe pumpkin?

Autumn festivals

In the UK and the USA, autumn happens towards the end of the year. Hallowe'en takes place on 31 October. People dress up as witches and ghosts.

Hallowe'en is a very popular event in the USA.

Remembrance Day in November
is when people remember those
who died in wars. Diwali is an
Indian and Nepalese festival held
in October or November.

Diwali is
also known
as the Festival
of Light.

Why do we have seasons?

We have seasons because Earth is tilted. As Earth moves around the Sun, different parts of the planet are nearer the Sun.

In **spring**, our part of the planet moves towards the Sun. The weather grows warmer.

In **summer**, our part of the planet is nearest the Sun. This means that the weather is hot.

In **autumn**, our part of the planet moves away from the Sun. The weather grows cooler.

In **winter**, our part of the planet is furthest from the Sun. This means that the weather is cold.

It takes a year for the four seasons to happen. This is because it takes a year for Earth to move around the Sun.

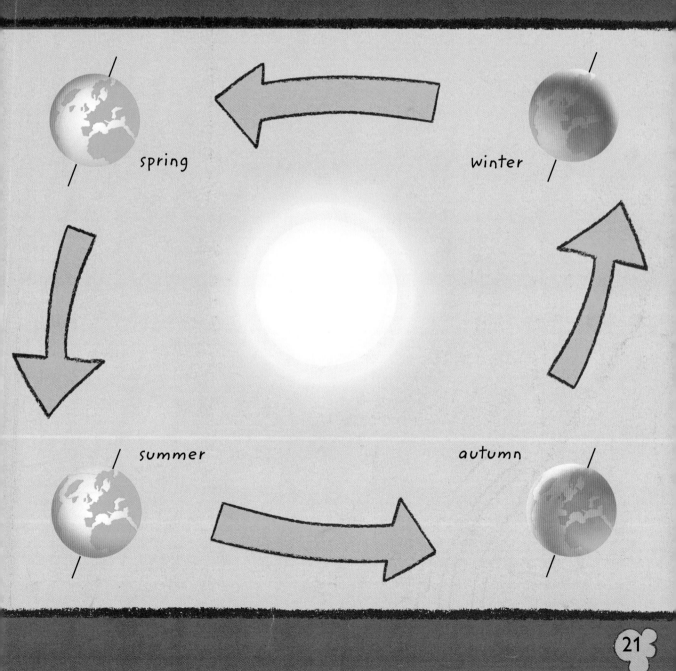

spring

winter

summer

autumn

Make a bird-seed feeder

Make a bird seed feeder to give the birds a healthy snack in autumn. You could leave out a shallow bowl of water for them, too.

1. Tie a piece of string around the middle of the pine cone. Make sure it's nice and tight.

2. Put the lard and mixture of dry ingredients into a bowl. Squeeze the mixture together with your fingers until you have a sticky mixture.

3. Carefully mould the mixture around the pine cone.

4. Put the pine cone in the fridge for an hour, so that the mixture goes hard.

5. Hang the bird seed feeder from a sturdy tree branch, and watch the feathery friends visit!

Glossary

blustery when wind is gusty and fierce

conker hard brown seed that grows on a horse chestnut tree

crop plants such as barley, wheat, corn and maize that are grown for food

foggy when the air is damp, misty and difficult to see through

frosty when it is cold and icy

grain seed such as corn and wheat that is used for making food

harvested when crops are gathered

horse chestnut tree a big tree that has seeds called conkers

Indian something that comes from the country called India

Nepalese something that comes from the country called Nepal

Index

animals 11, 12–13

birds 12, 22, 23

clothes 7

conkers 9, 15

crops 10–11

Earth 20, 21

festivals 18–19

food 11, 13, 16–17, 22, 23

kites 14

leaves 8, 15

pumpkin 17

spring 4, 9, 10, 20, 21

summer 4, 6, 20, 21

Sun 6, 20, 21

trees 8–9

weather 5, 6–7, 8, 12, 14, 20

windsurfing 14

winter 4, 13, 20, 21